Taro Gomi was born in Tokyo in
1945. In his very long career, he
has created more than 350 books
for readers of all ages. His work
has been translated into more than
15 languages, and among the 30
of his books to be published outside
of Japan are **Everyone Poops,
My Friends, Spring Is Here,
Scribbles,** and **Doodles.**

First published in the United States in 2007 by Chronicle Books LLC.

Copyright © 1996 by Taro Gomi.
Translation © 2007 by Chronicle Books LLC.
Originally published in Japan in 1996 under the title "NUTTARI KAITARI
RAKUGAKI BOOK" by Child Honsha Co., Ltd.
English translation rights arranged with Child Honsha Co., Ltd. through Japan
Foreign-Rights Centre.
All rights reserved.

Translation by Melissa Manlove.
English type design by Wendy Lui.
Typeset in Avenir.
Manufactured in China.
ISBN-13 978-0-8118-6151-9

10 9 8 7 6 5 4 3 2

Chronicle Books LLC
680 Second Street, San Francisco, California 94107

www.chroniclekids.com

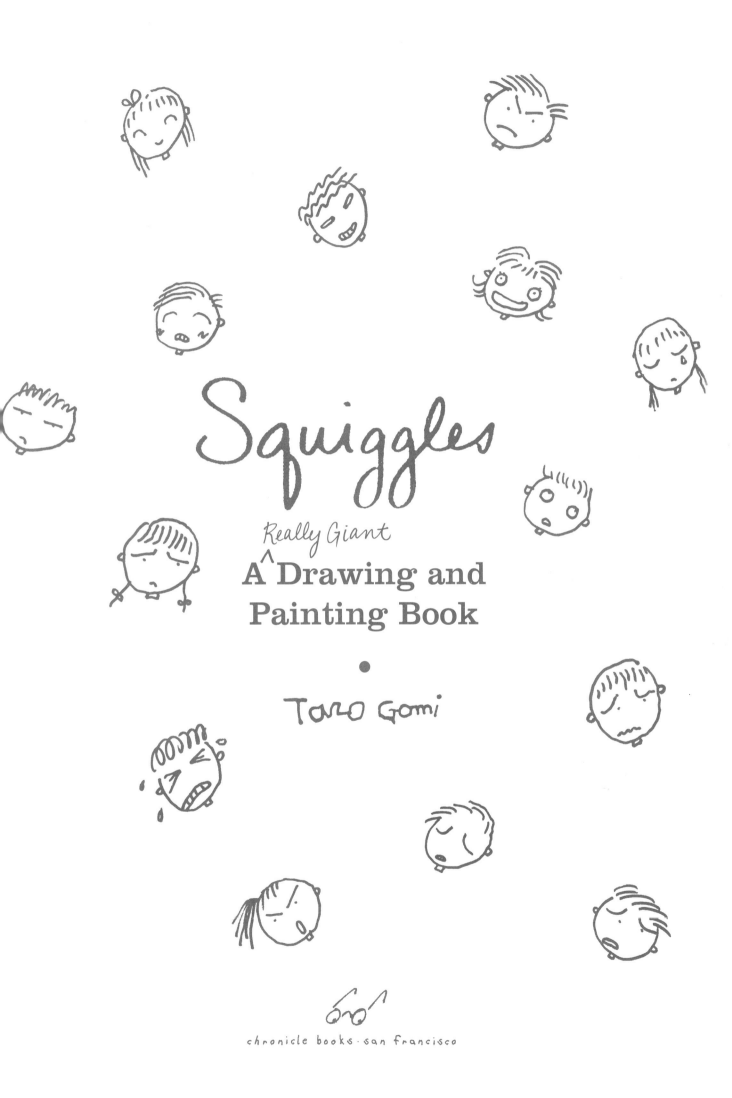

Squiggles

Really Giant
A^ Drawing and
Painting Book

•

Taro Gomi

chronicle books · san francisco

Some artists work quickly.
Some artists work slowly.
Some artists are very careful,
and some are very silly.
There are lots of kinds of artists.
But all artists like to play.
This book is full of ways to play.

Here *you* are the artist.

On this one, draw something that breathes water.

an adventure

Let's play in the mountains!

Paint people climbing mountains, camping, picnicking, maybe even skiing! Add some trees, flowers, and animals.

The mountains are getting higher and higher . . .

There are a lot of people in this scene.
Oops! There's been a little accident.

The landscape is turning into desert . . .

How does this adventure end?

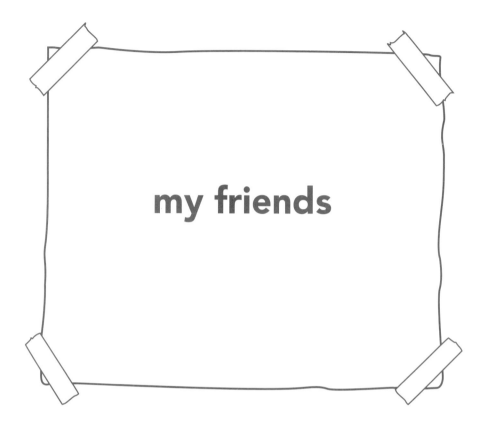

my friends

Give these people lots of different expressions.
Don't forget some funny hats.

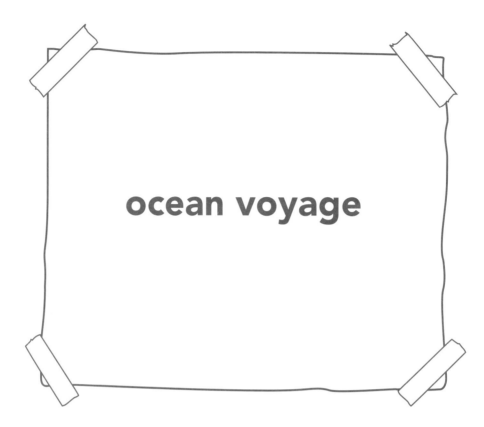

ocean voyage

Start with lots of fish.

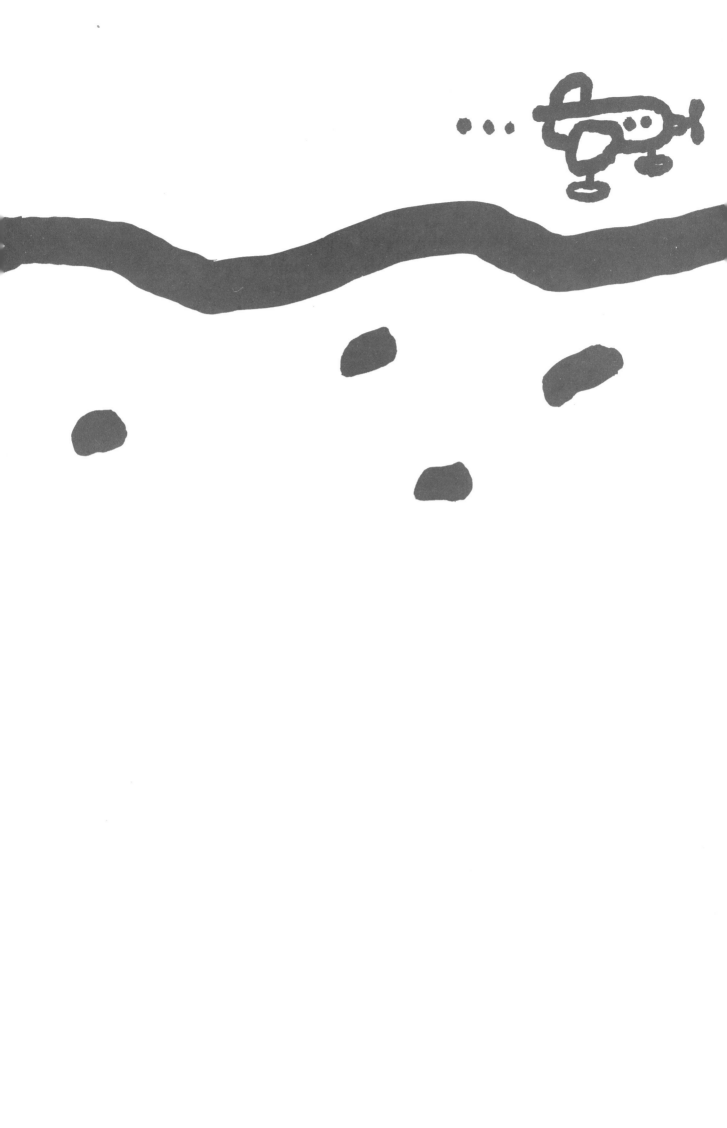

I'm sure there's some sunken treasure down here.
Maybe a sea monster, too.

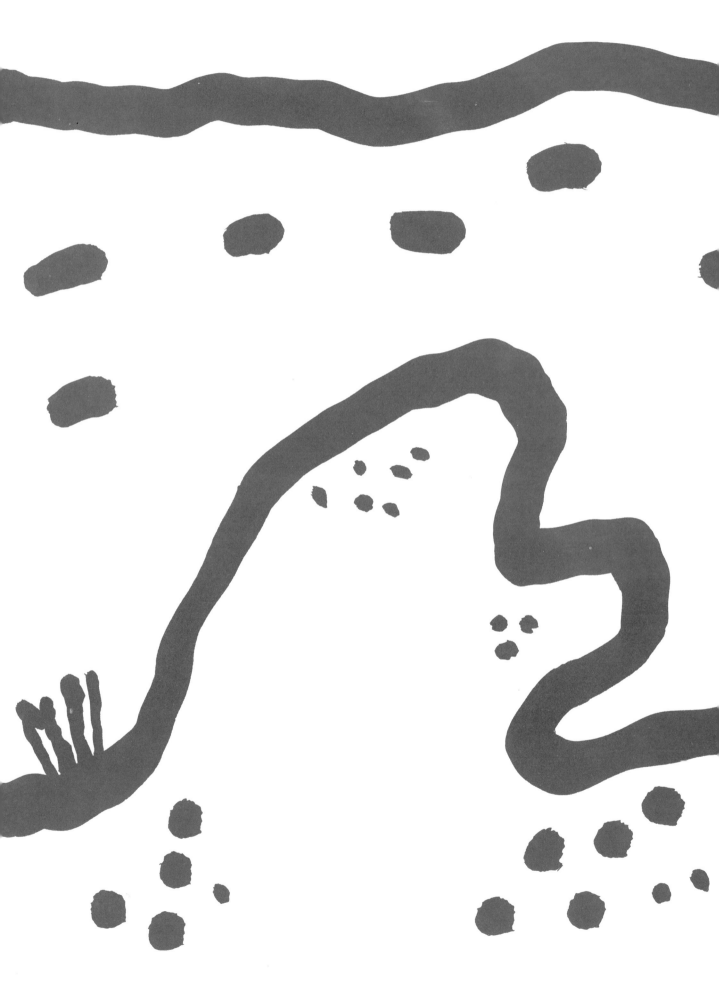

clothes & costumes

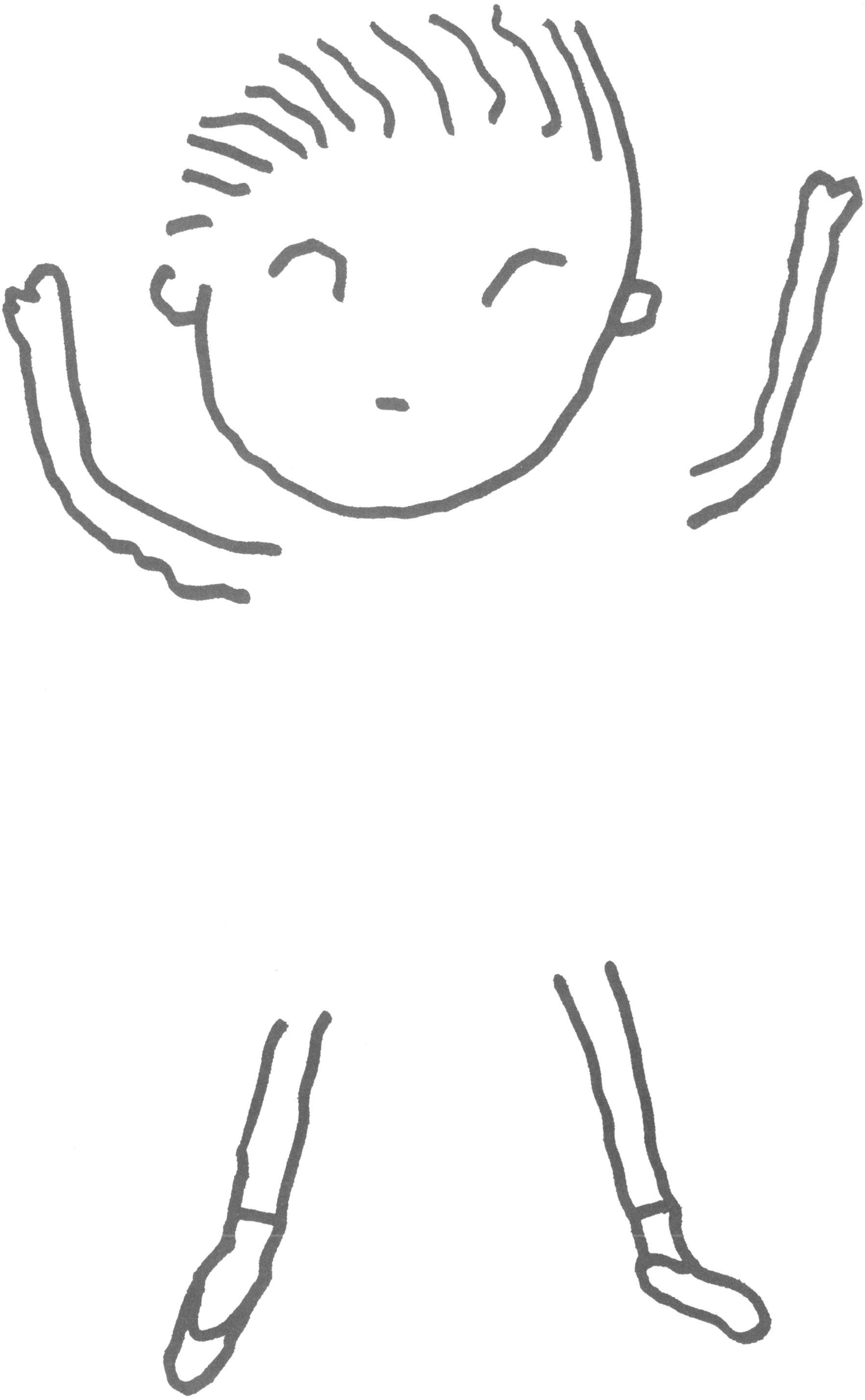

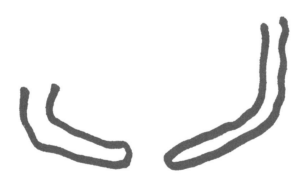

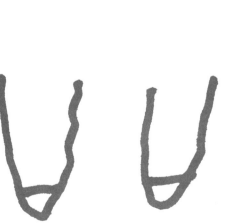

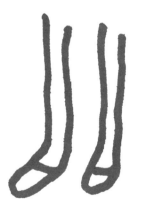

What kind of outfit completely covers the person wearing it?

time to eat!

This can be eaten with a spoon.

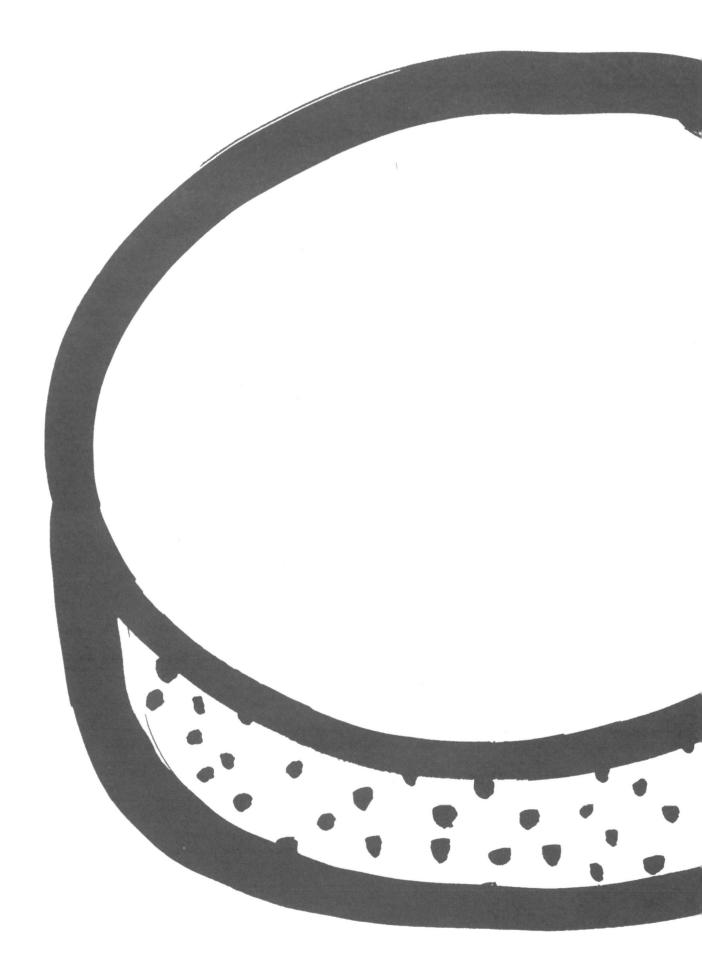

And this can be eaten with chopsticks.

This is going to be very difficult to eat.

Here are some more dishes to fill.

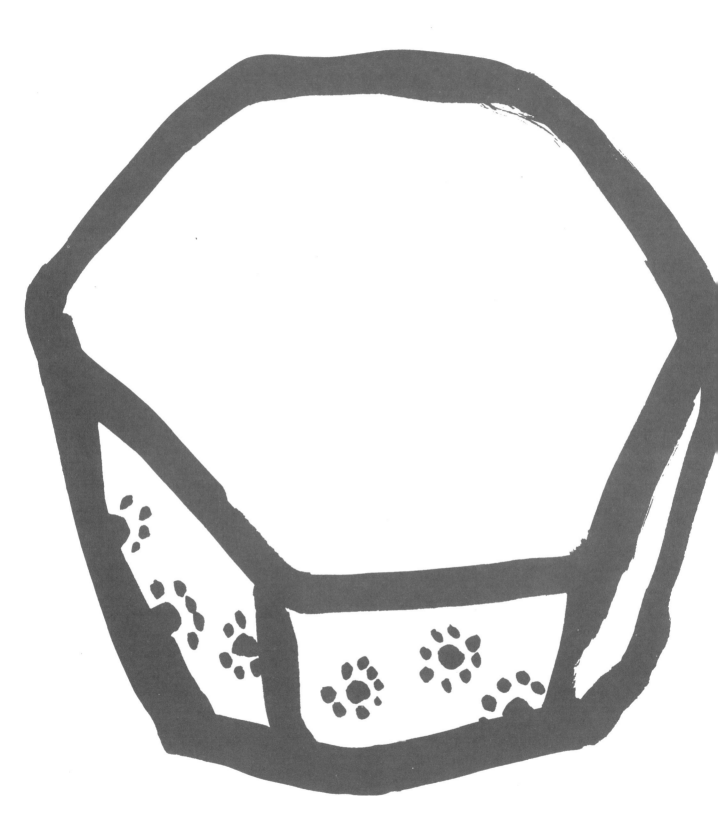

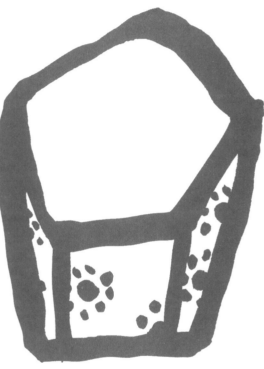

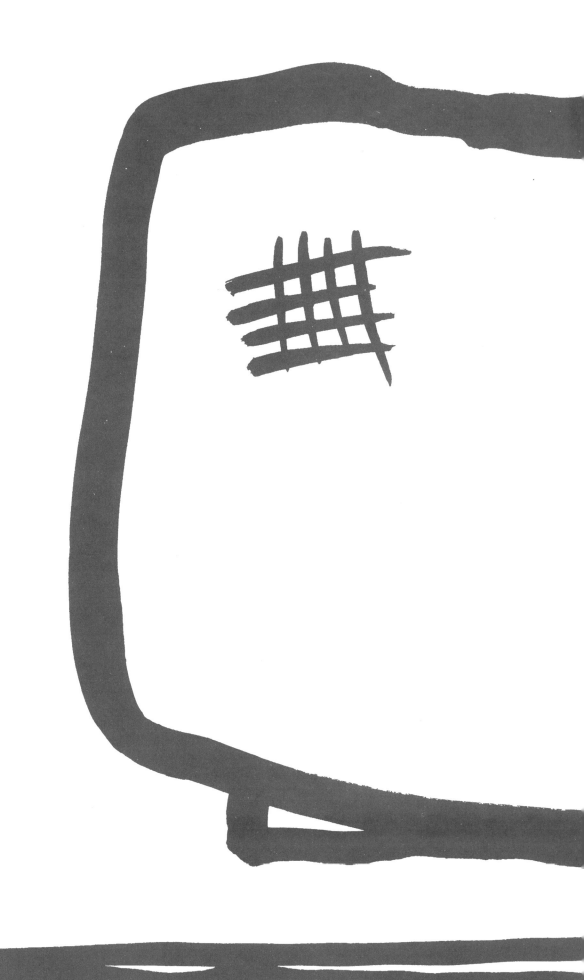

Oof! I'm full!

morning, noon,
and night

The sun is rising.

The sky is the most beautiful blue.

It's getting a little cloudy.

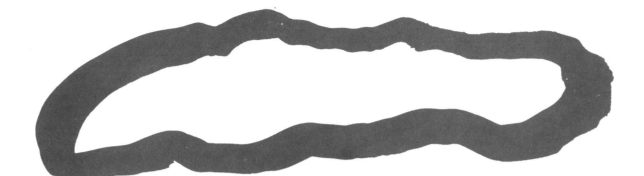

It's starting to rain.

Now it's getting very dark.

It's pouring.

Ooo, thunder and lightning!

Oh, good. The rain's stopping.

Now the sun is setting.

Good night.

Everyone is sleeping, except for the moon.

Everyone is sleeping, except for the moon.

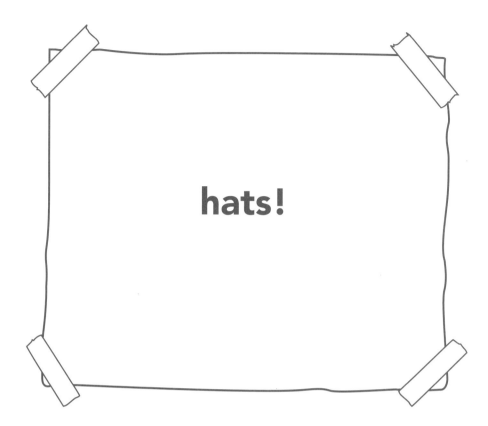

hats!

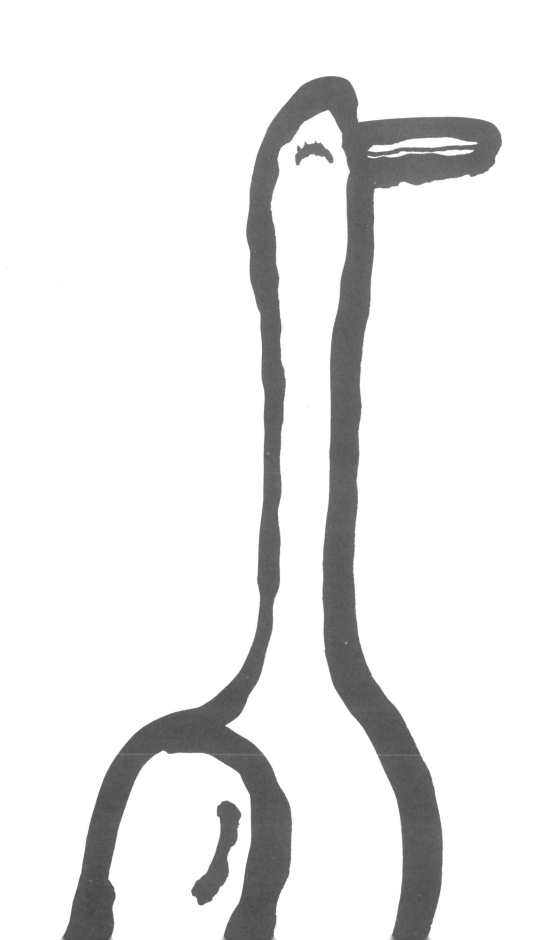

This one isn't a hat at all!

This one is just right.

This one is enormous!

vacation!

Who's in this car? (And what have they packed?)

And who's on this skateboard?

shopping!

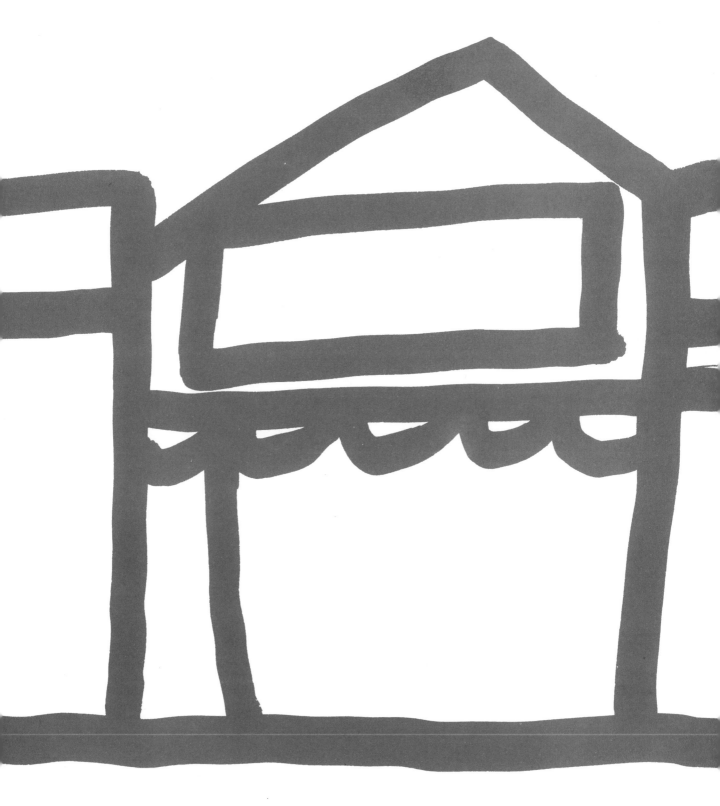

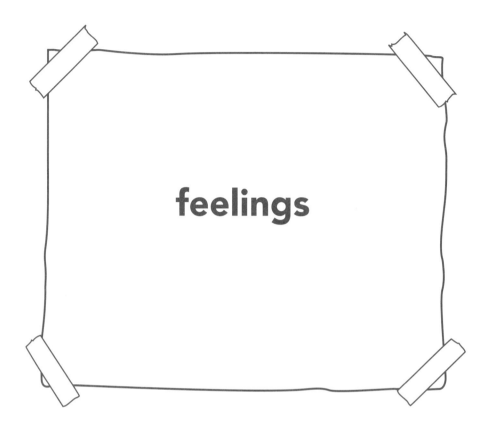

feelings

She's very happy.

"I'm sorry."

She's embarrassed.

"I'm not sure . . ."

"Ooo, I'm so angry!"

He's concentrating very hard.

"I'm a little scared."

He's making a funny face.

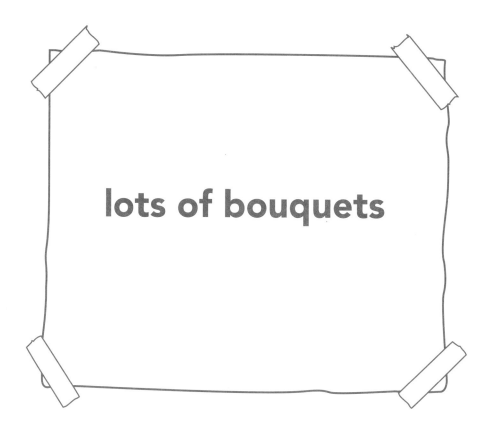

lots of bouquets

(Put some more flowers in this one.)

Put some frogs in this one.
(Well, it doesn't have to be frogs.)

These have wilted.

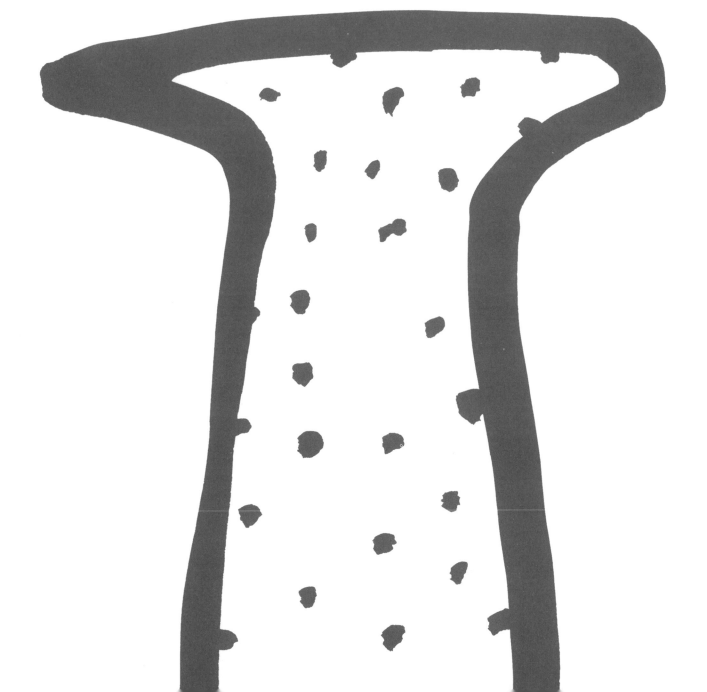

Perfect!

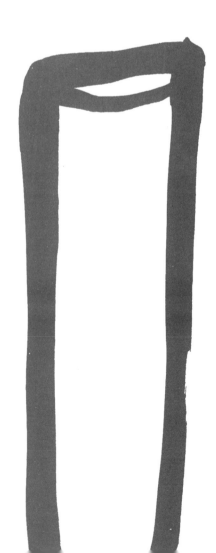